00121

121

First paperback edition 1998

First published 1995 in hardback by
A&C Black (Publishers) Limited,
35 Bedford Row, London WC1R 4JH

ISBN 0-7136-5019-2
A CIP catalogue record for this book is available
from the British Library.

Acknowledgements

Photographs by Zul Mukhida,
except pages 18 and 19; Eye Ubiquitous

Design by Helen White

Photographic and design direction by
Karen Bryant-Mole.

The author and publisher would like to thank all
the children who appear in the photographs.

They also wish to thank the Early Learning Centre,
Swindon for providing the equipment featured on
pages 8, 9, 16, 17 and the title page.

Printed and bound by Partenaires Fabrication,
Malesherbes, France.

Does it bounce?

Karen Bryant-Mole

A&C Black • London

go

Holly pedals her bike to make it **go**.

stop

When she puts her feet on the ground,
the bike **stops**.

float

Sam puts his boat in the water.
It **floats** on the top.

sink

Grace's car doesn't float.
It **sinks** to the bottom.

squeeze

When Yasmin **squeezes** the wet sponge,
water drips into the bucket.

spin

The clothes in Jess's washing machine
spin round and round.

lift

Grace has a toy telephone.
She **lifts** up the receiver.

press

She **presses** down the buttons
and pretends to call her friends.

heat

Holly's mum is **heating** up some milk
on the cooker.

cool

It's too hot!
Holly blows on it to **cool** it down.

twist

Sam **twists** the lid round to open the jar.

stir

Jess is making a cake.
She **stirs** the mixture with a big spoon.

backwards

Holly is trying to drive her jeep **backwards**.
Drive carefully, Holly!

forwards

It's much easier to drive **forwards**.

roll

Nahid **rolls** the ball along the ground.
Will he knock down the skittles?

bounce

Nahid loves **bouncing** up and down
on his trampoline.

fast

A racing car moves quickly.
It is very **fast**.

slow

A snail takes a long time to move.
It is **slow**.

push

Yasmin is **pushing** the wheelbarrow
in front of her.

pull

Now she is **pulling** the empty wheelbarrow
behind her.

throw

Jess is **throwing** a frisbee.
It will fly through the air.

catch

Grace **catches** the frisbee with both hands.

Index

This index will help you find the Buzzwords in this book.

backwards	14
bounce	17
catch	23
cool	11
fast	18
float	4
forwards	15
go	2
heat	10
lift	8
press	9
pull	21
push	20
roll	16
sink	5
slow	19
spin	7
squeeze	6
stir	13
stop	3
throw	22
twist	12

Things to do

Model
Make a model that can be pushed or pulled, that can go backwards or forwards, that can be fast or slow and that can go or stop. If you choose to make something on wheels, you could make a good base using an old shoe box. Push sticks through the box for axles and use cotton reels as wheels.

Play dough
See how many Buzzwords you can use when you play with play dough. Can you roll it, twist it, press it and squeeze it? Think of some other words, such as 'squash', that describe ways of playing with the play dough.

Floaters and sinkers
Make a collection of objects and see which objects float in water and which sink. A ball of Plasticine will sink. Can you find a way to change its shape and make it float?

Charades
This is a game you can play with your friends. Choose a Buzzword and act it out without speaking. Your friends have to guess which Buzzword you have chosen.

How to use this book

Children's understanding of concepts is fundamentally linked to their ability to comprehend and use relevant language. This book is designed to help children understand the vocabulary associated with forces.

Forces are an important area within science. They are one of the foundations upon which physics is built. Forces are responsible for the way an object moves or is moved.

Forces can be natural, like the push of water that enables an object to float, or manufactured, like the power of a car's engine. The movement of our own bodies can produce forces, such as a push on the handle of a pram.

Understanding the ways in which forces can act on objects is an essential scientific skill. Forces can push or pull things, can make things go or stop and can change the shape of things. This book helps children develop an understanding of this scientific concept by explaining key words connected with forces and by encouraging children to describe the actions that they make.

Some of the pairs of words featured on each double page are opposites, such as **fast** and **slow**. Other pairs of words, such as **twist** and **stir,** are not opposites. Children can be encouraged to think about the words and to discuss which pairs are opposites and which are not.

Each word in the book is explained through a colour photograph, which illustrates it, and a phrase, which uses that word in context. As well as explaining words that are basic to the understanding of forces, the book can be used in a number of other ways.

Children can think of situations, other than the one shown in the photograph, which can be described using a particular Buzzword. The Buzzword **go** does not just describe the movement of a bike. It can be applied to a wide variety of types of movement by many different sorts of objects. Cars, planes, boats, pushchairs, trains and horses all **go**.

Movements can often be described using more than one word. This book can help a child give a fuller description of a movement. The movement of a toy wheelbarrow, for instance, might be described using the words **go**, **forwards**, **push** and **slow**.

Forces also influence the shape of objects. Children can use some of the Buzzwords in this book to consider the ways in which they use forces in everyday activities. Clay can be twisted and stretched. Biscuit dough can be rolled and squeezed and wet sand can be pressed.